The 1,2,3 to Landing A Job!

The 1,2,3 to Landing A Job!

The 3 Steps to Getting Job Offers!

Griff Stevens,
BS, MBA, CLU, FLMI, ARA

iUniverse, Inc.
New York Lincoln Shanghai

The 1,2,3 to Landing A Job!
The 3 Steps to Getting Job Offers!

Copyright © 2006 by Griff Stevens

All rights reserved. No part of this book may be used or reproduced by any means, graphic, electronic, or mechanical, including photocopying, recording, taping or by any information storage retrieval system without the written permission of the publisher except in the case of brief quotations embodied in critical articles and reviews.

iUniverse books may be ordered through booksellers or by contacting:

iUniverse
2021 Pine Lake Road, Suite 100
Lincoln, NE 68512
www.iuniverse.com
1-800-Authors (1-800-288-4677)

The views expressed in this work are solely those of the author and do not necessarily reflect the views of the publisher, and the publisher hereby disclaims any responsibility for them.

ISBN-13: 978-0-595-41461-1 (pbk)
ISBN-13: 978-0-595-85810-1 (ebk)
ISBN-10: 0-595-41461-3 (pbk)
ISBN-10: 0-595-85810-4 (ebk)

Printed in the United States of America

CONTENTS

INTRODUCTION vii

STEP 1—COMPLETE A PROFESSIONAL RESUME' 1
    RESUME' SAMPLE 4

STEP 2—PREPARE FOR INTERVIEWING 7
    DECIDE WHAT YOU WANT TO DO 7
    RESEARCH COMPANIES PRIOR TO INTERVIEWING 9
    QUESTIONS TO BE PREPARED TO ANSWER IN
    INTERVIEWS 10
    QUESTIONS TO BE PREPARED TO ANSWER IN
    INTERVIEWS; SUGGESTED ANSWERS 12
    QUESTIONS TO ASK IN INTERVIEWS 27

STEP 3—BEGIN TO APPROACH THE JOB MARKET 34
    NETWORKING 35
    NETWORK CONTACT REPORT 36
    NETWORK LETTER TO YOUR COMPANIES—1st LETTER 38
    NETWORK FOLLOWUP CALL GUIDELINES 40
    NETWORK MEETING GUIDELINES 41
    NETWORK THANK YOU LETTER 43

NETWORK FOLLOW-UP LETTER 45

NETWORK INTERVIEW REQUEST LETTER 47

ISSUING RESUMES' 49

ISSUING RESUMES' EMPLOYER DIRECT LETTER 50

ISSUING RESUMES' INTERVIEW FOLLOW-UP 51

ISSUING RESUMES' APPLICATION FOLLOW-UP 52

ISSUING RESUMES' CALL FOLLOW-UP 53

ISSUING RESUMES' DELAY FOLLOW-UP 54

SEARCH FIRM CONTACTS 55

SEARCH FIRM CONTACT CALL GUIDELINES 56

SEARCH FIRM CONTACT FOLLOW-UP LETTER 57

PPLA, Inc., JOB HUNTING SERVICES APPLICATION 58

EPILOGUE 59

PROFESSIONAL & PERSONAL LIVING ASSISTANTS, INC. 69

INTRODUCTION

In a career that has spanned over twenty-five years I have worked for six different companies and held approximately fifteen different managerial roles at first line supervisory, mid-management, and executive levels. I was made an Assistant Vice President of a small financial firm in 1992 at the age of thirty-six and by the age of forty had achieved a six-figure income. By my standards, I've done OK.

But through all the failures and successes, there was still something missing that I needed to accomplish in my career. So I created an organization called "Professional and Personal Living Assistants", Inc., and went to work helping people in some of the aspects of their lives we all seem to find a bit challenging. One of these aspects is the challenge of job-hunting.

I've studied the art of job-hunting for over twenty years. I simply thought that the only thing really missing in the marketplace was a very concise "how do I get started", "how do I go about it" and "how do I really land the job I want", kind of book. So, that is what I've written. To me, there are simply three steps in job-hunting, and they are;

Completing a professional resume'.

Preparing for interviewing.

Approaching the job market.

This book tells you how to go about it, gives numerous examples covering each step, and leads you through the process. Specific information is provided on how to construct your resume', how to prepare for interviewing, and how to approach the market.

The resume' section gives specifics on what sections a resume' should contain and key musts that will set your resume' apart from others. The interviewing section provides numerous questions you must be prepared to answer and questions to ask so you can interview the company as well. The last section, approaching the job market, provides you with the actual techniques needed to give you the best shot at opening a company's door. These include a system for logging information, distributing mailings, follow-up calls, and most importantly what to say in both these written and verbal contacts.

Just as important as all the specifics and directions that are provided, are the numerous "rationale" sections throughout the book. The reader is strongly encouraged to take the "rationale" sections to heart and realize this information is based on years of interviewing, hiring, firing, and market analysis experience.

So, whether you are a seasoned professional, an entry level employee, a highly paid executive, industry worker, office worker, career changer, or recent college graduate, this book will help shape your outlook on job hunting and give you the mindset and tools you can take to any job search campaign.

If after reading my book you are still in need of assistance in writing your resume', preparing for interviewing, or approaching the job market, please visit our website at "pplaservicesforyou.com". Professional & Personal Living Assistants, Inc. provides additional services that can get you on the right track.

The ultimate goal of my book is that after reading it you will walk away forever more confident in your ability to land a job, knowing you now have a process and a system you can employ at any time when finding a job is imperative.

So, without further fanfare, and as is my style throughout this book, let's get right down to it! I only have one more thing to add before we get started. I do know for a fact that this book can help you in your efforts to land a job. I have proven it in working with many friends and associates. I know that you too can make it happen if you are sincerely motivated and dedicated. I wish you the best of luck in all your career endeavors.

STEP 1
COMPLETE A PROFESSIONAL RESUME'

1. RESUMES' SHOULD <u>ONLY</u> INCLUDE THE FOLLOWING SECTIONS:
   A. GENERAL SUMMARY
   B. POSITION OBJECTIVE
   C. BUSINESS EXPERIENCE
   D. EDUCATION

   RATIONALE:
   Resumes' should be all business. Employers want people who'll get the job done!

   A. "GENERAL SUMMARY"
      This is a brief description of your education and experience highlighting your key professional areas of expertise. It is important to keep this section brief!

      RATIONALE:
      Hopefully these highlights will match the employer's needs and they will immediately be interested in reading further! Being brief is important so they can see your expertise easily.

   B. "POSITION OBJECTIVE"
      Either the exact name of the position being sought or a very brief objective should be stated. While I prefer the exact name of the position being sought, I've provided a few brief objective examples below;

      "A position where my experience in Customer Relations and Operations Management, supported by innovative decision-making will result in a more efficient and effective organization."

OR
"A position where my advanced organizational, management, and analytical skills can be utilized to the fullest, allowing me to contribute to the organization's success."

RATIONALE:
Objectives should be short and sweet, because the best objective you can offer is a general one. Don't belabor the point, but rather just state your interest in the position. I personally prefer the use of a "position objective" just providing the name of the job you are after.

C. "BUSINESS EXPERIENCE"
Should consist of the following sections:
1. Key responsibilities broken down into sub-sections that match the highlighted areas of expertise you began with in your general summary.
2. Accomplishments—This area is a **MUST** and should highlight the key accomplishments you've achieved while employed with the organization. The accomplishments should be viewed as your opportunity to show the employer why you are different and better than other candidates! Whenever possible, you should include specific numbers highlighting the degree of your success, for example; "I achieved a **20%** quality improvement."

D. "EDUCATION"
This section should show all educational achievements. If you have numerous achievements that begin to make this section too large, limit it to only displaying what is pertinent to the job you want.

2. OVERALL GUIDELINES:

A. A resume' should be kept as brief as possible and **NEVER** go over 2 pages in length. (The resume' sample provided in this book exceeds 2 pages only due to the reduced book margins.)

RATIONALE:
Employers and/or Managers reviewing resumes are busy people. They don't have time to read your life story. The single purpose of the resume' is to show you have the skills and experience to do the job

and to open the door getting you an interview for the position, **PERIOD!**

B. If you are having trouble coming up with the right wording and/or just are not confident in your writing abilities, try these suggestions:

  I. Have friends, associates, and peers read your resume'. Get honest feedback and make appropriate changes.

  II. Use the same words from job advertisements and/or descriptions of the jobs you are going after.

4 The 1,2,3 to Landing A Job!

RESUME' SAMPLE
THOMAS JOHNSON
100 Johnson Street
St. Louis, MO 63103
999-999-9999 (Home)
888-888-8888 Ext. 8888 (Work)
777-777-7777 (Cell)

<u>GENERAL SUMMARY:</u> Management professional with extensive experience in CUSTOMER RELATIONS, OPERATIONS MANAGEMENT, TRAINING, MARKETING RESEARCH, AND SYSTEMS DEVELOPMENT. Hold BS and MBA Degrees in Business and Management.

<u>POSITION OBJECTIVE:</u> Operations Manager

BUSINESS EXPERIENCE:

Safe Way Insurance Company, Inc.—St. Louis, MO (May 2004–Present)
<u>MARKETING SERVICES, COMPETITIVE & TRENDS RESEARCH ANALYST</u>
Responsible for leading marketing department in two key areas; one to provide insight regarding new trends to ensure the organization is looking forward and second to ensure products are competitive when entering new markets. Major responsibilities involve:
<u>Business & Competitive Analysis</u>—Analyzing pertinent competition and new industry trends and providing feedback verbally, in written documents, and through informal and formal presentations to all company departments as needed.
<u>Customer Relations</u>—Ensuring auto club members, insurance customers, and vendors are provided excellent service.
<u>Accomplishments</u>—Organized the development of three product specification documents for Memberships, Auto, and Homeowners Insurance and assisted in the development of new homeowners' output forms.

Insurance Software Products, Inc.—St. Louis, MO (July 2001–May 2004)
<u>CLIENT SERVICES, BUSINESS CONSULTANT—SOFTWARE DEVELOPMENT</u>
Responsible for assisting in the development, successful installation, and on-going service of the corporations' reinsurance software product for both nationally and internationally based clients. Major responsibilities involved:
<u>Customer Relations Management</u>—Ensured system modifications were completed in a timely manner, installations were completed according to schedule, and provided effective on-going service to newly developed client base.
<u>Systems Design</u>—Responsible for assisting in the developing of a reliable system modified to the client's expectations in order to meet their processing needs. This included analysis of overall system functionality, response times, report output, systems modification needs, analysis, and testing, and determining the systems overall impact on the client's efficiency.

RESUME SAMPLE—page 2
THOMAS JOHNSON
100 Johnson Street
St. Louis, MO 63103
999-999-9999 (Home)
888-888-8888 Ext. 8888 (Work)
777-777-7777 (Cell)

Accomplishments—Assisted with development and completion of over 50 system modifications for the company's first major client. Provided client support and training on system functionality for company's parent company installation.

Insurance for Insurance Company's, Inc.—St. Louis, MO (Oct. 1998–July 2001)
DIRECTOR—REINSURANCE ADMINISTRATION
Responsible for administration of the company's reinsurance products marketed worldwide. Major responsibilities involved:
Customer Relations Management—Maintained strict adherence to treaty agreements, oversaw processing of 868 MIL in annualized premiums, and maintained effective client service for client base of 400+ companies.
Accomplishments—Documented processing procedures and established an electronic workflow processing status system.

Towers Insurance Co.—St. Louis, MO (Jan. 1988–Oct. 1998)
DIRECTOR of CUSTOMER RELATIONS
Responsible for managing the service department supporting the company's group and individual universal and variable universal life products marketed nationally. Major responsibilities involved
Operations Management—Maintained corporate service standards, to include adherence to established underwriting policy, timely applications processing, claims analysis and payment approval, application of 85 MIL in annualized premiums, and maintained effective customer service for 150+ group clients and over 75,000 policyholder's country wide.
Accomplishments—Built a successful service operation in seven years, handpicking the entire staff and provided training on operations procedures and administrative systems. The company grew from 4 MIL to 85 MIL in annual premiums. Also assisted in and coordinated the conversion of several mainframe computer systems operations reducing system costs by $125,000 annually, substantially improved productivity, and effectively managed the departments 1.3 MIL dollar budget.

Washington National Insurance Co.—St. Louis, MO (Aug. 1985–Jan. 1988)
I.T. OPERATIONS MANAGER (7/87–1/88)
Responsible for directing senior management in the acquisition of new technologies. Major responsibilities included handling installation of new technologies and coordinating special project communications between the information technology team and the user areas.

RESUME SAMPLE—page 3
THOMAS JOHNSON
100 Johnson Street
St. Louis, MO 63103
999-999-9999 (Home)
888-888-8888 Ext. 8888 (Work)
777-777-7777 (Cell)

OPERATIONS MANAGER (8/85–7/87)
Managed the operations department of a growing (100+ MIL in A.P.) insurance company. Major responsibilities involved:
Operations management—Maintaining service standards along with developing and maintaining the department's 1.6 million dollar budget. Managed 45 employees: 5 management/40 staff.
Accomplishments—Restructured key operating units resulting in a 7% increase in productivity and revised the quote generation and cash application systems achieving a 15% improvement in productivity.

Wisconsin Home Insurance Companies, Inc.—St. Louis, MO (Sept. 1979–Aug. 1985)
Held a variety of first line supervisory positions. Major responsibilities included directing and controlling staff activities to ensure daily production and quality of work standards were achieved. Held supervisory positions in areas such as Customer Service, Endorsements, Assigned Risk, Mailing, and Filing.
Accomplishments—Developed a department-wide motivational program titled "AIM", a synonym for All Individuals Motivated. Program resulted in $300,000 annual savings. Staffed, and supervised a new unit that achieved a 22% improvement in timeliness of cash applications. Assisted in testing and verification of a new systems conversion.

OTHER TRAINING ACCOMPLISHMENTS:
Taught a weekend "Administrative Management" class for Johnstown University.
Presently teach a weekend "Life Insurance Licensing Certification" class for All America, a position I have held for 7 years.
Presently teach a "Principles of Insurance & Risk Management" class for Southern University, a position held for 4 years.
Provided training for numerous staff members in different environments regarding new systems functionality and upgrades.

EDUCATION:

M.B.A. Degree-Management, Northern College	B.S. Degree-Business, University of Idaho
Series 6 and 63 licensed	Property and Casualty insurance licensed
Health and Life insurance licensed	Fellow in Life Management Institute (FLMI)
Associate, Reinsurance Administration (ARA)	Certified Life Underwriter (CLU)

STEP 2
PREPARE FOR INTERVIEWING

There Are Four Steps In The Interview Preparation Process:

1. **DECIDE WHAT YOU WANT TO DO**
    A. For example, a previous individual I worked with decided they wanted:
        I. To work in a positive no-nonsense environment & charitable organization.
        II. To work with other professionals knowledgeable in their field.
        III. To work with people open to change and dedicated to working as a team.
        IV. To contribute to a company, which becomes a leader in the industry.
        V. To develop and manage a positive, dedicated staff.
        VI. To work with people who respect each other for their knowledge and expertise.
        VII. To work for a small company, one with less than fifty employees.

        RATIONALE:
        It is very important to show direction and determination when interviewing for any position. If you accomplish anything in an interview, make sure of one thing; the employer knows you want their job!!!

        You should really take time to reflect on what you really want from your work. Make a list, make a plan, and go for it!

OTHER HELPFUL HINTS:
If you're having any trouble deciding on what it is you really want to do, try these books, which will really get you thinking:

I DON'T KNOW WHAT I WANT BUT I KNOW IT'S NOT THIS
By Julie Jensen

CHANGE YOUR JOB, CHANGE YOUR LIFE
By Ron Krannich

WHAT COLOR IS YOUR PARACHUTE
By Richard Nelson Bolles

2. **RESEARCH COMPANIES PRIOR TO INTERVIEWING**
   A. Company's major source of income—via an annual report
   B. Company's financial situation; challenges, growth rate, etcetera, via
      1. Value Line Investment Survey
      2. Sorkins
   C. Company's Reputation and Industry Ranking, via
      1. Investment Broker
      2. Everybody's Business
      3. Dunn & Bradstreet's Reference Book of Corporate Management
      4. Standard & Poors Register of Corporations, Directors, & Executives.
   D. Other Company Information desired via
      1. Directory of Corporations
      2. Career Guide to Professional Organizations
      3. National Trade & Professional Associations
      4. Encyclopedia of Associations
      5. Contacts Influential

   RATIONALE:
   The amount of research you should perform is directly proportional to your level of interest in a particular position. While not completely critical in this process, if you are very interested in a company you can display that interest by knowing as much as possible about them prior to your interview.

   NOTE:
   The kind of information you may want to find out about an organization could include growth rate, where the growth is coming from, total net income, profitability, number of years they have been in business, number of employees, company's reputation, number of competitors, most dangerous competitors, types of professionals employed, etcetera. You may find and/or add other information you want from the sources above. If researching a company is important to you, you will want to get to know the aforementioned publications, and subsequently get to know what they can provide. You can find these sources on-line or at any university or business library.

3. **QUESTIONS TO BE PREPARED TO ANSWER IN INTERVIEWS**

BE ABLE TO:
- A. State your cost or present net worth, including salary, benefits, and perks.
- B. Provide a list of references; Personal and Business—three of each.
- C. Describe what you have done and what you do.
- D. Explain type of person you are; goals, personality, strengths & weaknesses.
- E. Explain why you have come to them and what you can contribute.
- F. Describe the perfect job.
- G. Succinctly detail five and ten year plans.
- H. Explain how you obtained your last job and/or previous jobs.
- I. Explain why you did or did not want to leave your last job(s).
- J. Describe what you liked or disliked about your last job(s).
- K. Describe your greatest professional and/or job accomplishment.
- L. Describe what your last supervisor was like.
- M. Describe difficult things you had to do on your last job(s).
- N. Explain why you attended the college you selected.
- O. State leisure activities, which provide the most satisfaction.
- P. Explain things that you and your last supervisor disagreed on.
- Q. Describe your last supervisor's greatest strengths.
- R. Describe areas you felt your supervisor could have done a better job.
- S. Explain how your last supervisor treated you.
- T. Describe ways in which your supervisor developed your skills.
- U. Describe the type of supervisor you feel you work best for.
- V. Describe the job duties, which gave you the most satisfaction.
- W. Describe the job duties, which gave you the least satisfaction.
- X. Explain the progress you have made with your present company.
- Y. Explain what you expect out of a job.
- Z. Explain what you expect from the company who hires you.

AA. Relay how long you have been searching for this type of job.
AB. Describe your outstanding qualities.
AC. Describe areas you feel you need improvement.
AD. Explain why you would like to work for their company.
AE. Describe what you think determines an employee's progress in a company.
AF. Describe a situation when you organized a project.
AG. Describe a situation when you disciplined an employee.
AH. Describe a time when you handled a difficult situation.

RATIONALE:

The marketplace is competitive. There were probably fifty to one hundred resumes' and many qualified candidates for this position. Your ability to present yourself as the best candidate for the position comes down to your ability to handle the interview! It is very important that answers to possible questions have been thought out and are succinct.

QUESTIONS TO BE PREPARED TO ANSWER IN INTERVIEWS; SUGGESTED ANSWERS

Before you take a look at this section, please note that under each of the questions I have provided what I have termed the "Possible Meaning." I've done this for two reasons. One, you could be asked any of these questions in multiple ways and the "Possible Meaning" gives you a possible alternative to how the interviewer may ask the question. And two, I wanted to stimulate in you a deeper analysis in regards to what an interviewer may really be asking. Please review the "Possible Meaning" items and reflect and compare them to the listed question. My hope is that it gets you to really think about what you want to say when answering any question.

BE ABLE TO:

    A.   State your cost or present net worth, including salary, benefits, and perks.
Possible Meaning: What will it take to get you to come to work here?
Be able to state what income level you need or desire. The typical rule of thumb is not to bring up the compensation issue until the very end of the interview process. When the employer brings it up make sure you are ready. You should state your requirement in the form of a range, for example; $30,000 to $35,000 per year. Typically, the more you want, the bigger the range; $75,000 to $85,000, and so forth. The most important thing to remember is that you should not bring up this issue until asked. If you are a dedicated professional your number one interest and focus is on what can be accomplished and whether you will be allowed to use your skills and abilities to make a difference. When the job gets done, smart employers will pay the effective professional well.

    B.   Provide a list of references; Personal and Business—three of each.
Possible Meaning: Does this candidate have the respect of peers and friends?
Be sure to include complete names, home addresses, office phone numbers, and cellular phone numbers if possible.

C. Describe what you have done and what you do.
Possible Meaning: Does this candidate get excited about his or her work, and/or does he or she have any solid accomplishments, and/or can he or she communicate well?

Don't ramble on and on and on if you are asked this question. However, on the other hand, you must be able to explain what you have done and what you've accomplished. I get good at this by memorizing my resume', starting with my oldest position and working my way back to the most current position. But it is important to keep it succinct. For example, I might say the following in regards to a customer service management position.

"I coordinated the efforts of a twenty member team dedicated to ensuring a high level of customer satisfaction. We didn't lose one account while I managed this team."

The key is to not over do it, but to remain focused on summarizing to the best of your ability what you have done in each position and challenges you have faced. Don't forget to throw in some accomplishments if the question is asked in terms of what you have done or accomplished. Remember, this question may present the opportunity for you to brag about some of your accomplishments. Hopefully you are proud of some of the things you've done—so let the employer know!

D. Explain type of person you are; goals, personality, strengths & weaknesses.
Possible Meaning: Does this candidate have any goals and do they tie in with our goals? Will this person's personality, strengths, and weaknesses blend well with our company culture?

This is a challenging question or series of questions, to say the least. You must analyze yourself and your goals, and be ready with a list of at least three to five items for each of the categories above. For starters, your goals should specify where you want to be in five or ten years in terms of compensation, position, responsibilities, and any other items that are important to you. Obviously you must be realistic or you could easily remove yourself from contention by setting unrealistic goals the company is unable to help you achieve. Regarding personality, you should be ready with an honest appraisal of yourself and a few attributes that describe you. For instance; Upbeat and positive, good listener, and easy to communicate with are traits I sometimes use. For strengths, I'd come ready with at least five. I like to use, very hard working, very self-motivated, very detail minded and thorough, versatile, and extremely organized. For weaknesses you need to be careful. This question can make you look bad if you describe too many, and arrogant if you provide too few or none. I like to go with some I consider to be double edged and can in reality make you look good. For instance, I like to use impatience in getting things done. I state that I can get a little frustrated if the company is slow to really make things happen. You can see how an employer that really does want to make things happen, may be thinking this candidate will fit right in! Another I like to use is "moving too fast" and having to re-do work or go back to complete the item or project. While this can be a little dangerous you can qualify it by saying that you don't really cause problems, but rather just more work for yourself. Whatever weaknesses you use, you should think them through, qualify them if need be, and make sure they can be seen through as potential strengths.

E. Explain why you have come to them and what you can contribute.
Possible Meaning: Does this candidate really want to work here and can he or she add value?

This is pretty straightforward. If you are able to say that you've researched their company, and you know they are growing which to you equates to opportunity, plus you enjoy the kind of work they are offering, then you may be putting yourself a step above other candidates who have no specific response. I did say earlier the amount of research you do will be directly related to your amount of interest in a particular position, so let's assume you've not done any. Without any research you might try stating that you know they have a good reputation and you desire to stay in your community. This is a decent response albeit you must be ready for a tough interviewer asking how you know they have a good reputation. Like I've shared several times in this book; always be ready to support any statement you make! The "what can you contribute" part of this question should tie into your strengths, skills, and experience and should draw on all of these to specify how you can help them. For instance, you might say that you've been involved in very detailed oriented projects, you know quality of work is very important to them, and you believe you have good abilities to do very thorough work and/or spot errors and help maintain a quality product.

F. Describe the perfect job.
    Possible Meaning: Are this candidate's interests truly a match with the duties and responsibilities of our position?

    A tough question if what you are applying for is not your dream job. You must be careful not to describe something the position you are going for cannot offer. Stick with generalities stating things such as "a job where I can truly contribute to the companies success," a position where I can utilize my strong organizational skills or a position where all team members are dedicated to making great things happen and management and staff work in unison."

G. Succinctly detail five and ten year plans.
    Possible Meaning: Do the candidate's short and long term goals match with the organizations and can we help him or her achieve them? What level of position does this candidate expect to obtain, and when?

    We discussed this briefly prior to this question, but you should know where you want to go and that many employers like asking this. Make sure you have thought about it and decided on some key questions in your own professional growth; like do you want management responsibilities, do you want to remain in the area your selecting now or do you see yourself moving to another department, and do you have specific income goals? You should know where you want to go!

H. Explain how you obtained your last job and/or previous jobs.
    Possible Meaning: Is this person a self-starter? Has he or she made things happen on his or her own?

    Make sure you can relay this story for each and every job you've ever held. Employers like to know if you've obtained positions on your own or had assistance along the way. The standard answers are obvious; networking, newspaper advertisement, on-line research, and others discussed in this book.

I. Explain why you did or did not want to leave your last job(s).
    Possible Meaning: Were there any problems connected with your departure from any of your previous employers?

    Be ready to explain very succinctly and positively why you have left every position you've held. If there is a negative story involved in any departure, keep it as brief as possible and present it as past history with no affect on your future. For instance, I once left an organization due to the sweeping lack of work ethic permeating throughout the company coupled with a very power hungry regime, which made most decisions based on political beliefs and policies, not what was truly right and best for the organization. Did you notice how negative the last sentence sounded? I did that on purpose to show how never to answer any question in an interview. There is nothing in that answer that I would ever share with a prospective employer. While what I said above was true about that employer, here's how I answer why I left them, which by the way, I have been asked on many occasions. I simply say that the company went through a reorganization; eliminating the original unit I had been hired to run and moved me to another department. The new department was slow to move and more bureaucratic, and I was bored. This was all true by the way, and as you can see I simply focus on another approach to answering this question.

J. Describe what you liked or disliked about your last job(s).
Possible Meaning: Are you a dedicated employee that stays focused on objectives and allows very little to deter you from adding value?

Once again focus on the positives. Always keep in mind employers are looking for positive problem solvers that can get the job done and make great things happen. Along the lines of dislikes I might use something such as, "I disliked that most decisions were upper management directives with little feedback provided from lower management levels."

While this is a dangerous response if that is presently the motif operandi of this organization, I feel strongly about contributing and can make many of the necessary decisions. I don't need someone always doing that for me, and probably don't want this position if that is how most decisions are made. So, in this case, I may want to learn how this organization operates. As I said, the best and safest approach is to focus on "likes" such as, my boss was very interested in everyone's professional development, management was very attuned helping their staff achieve objectives, or we were a growing company that went through many changes. You should have at least three likes and dislikes for every job you have held, and select those that present you in the best way to the employer. Always remember the motto of answering interviewing questions; **"BE PREPARED."**

K. Describe your greatest professional and/or job accomplishment.
Possible Meaning: What does this individual really like to do? What is he or she proudest of and does it relate to what we need to accomplish?

This will hopefully be something that will relate well to the responsibilities of the position you are interviewing for. Let your genuine enthusiasm and pride come out and display for the prospective employer how you get excited, pumped up, and into your work, and as important, your accomplishments. If you don't have anything specific to relay, or anything you consider major, at least share something you believe was a success. For instance, you might share that my boss and I were a great team and together we got it done, day in and day out! Not saying anything to this question would be the kiss of death. The employer wants to know that you get involved in your work and enjoy success and doing a good job.

L. Describe what your last supervisor was like.
Possible Meaning: What traits do you like in a supervisor and/or does this person stay positive even when the supervisor doesn't?

Be ready with a brief description of any previous supervisors especially the latest ones. Your description should be brief and include items such as fair, tough, demanding, honest, caring, professional, dedicated, hard-working, etcetera. You can throw in some negatives if you want to make it more realistic, but keep in mind that throughout the interview process, whenever you make any statement, you must be able to back it up or elaborate in a positive manner. For instance, you might have said your last boss overall was very good, except that he or she was a poor communicator. The interviewer might come back with a question asking if you could provide an example or two of why he or she was a poor communicator. You must be prepared for this after any statement you make and in this case you might state that he or she often asked me to attend, or called me into meetings spontaneously. It would have been nice to have had time to prepare. I could have contributed more if I was able to prepare. Be careful taking this path, but realize being very open and honest in an interview can help.

M. Describe difficult things you had to do on your last job(s).
Possible Meaning: Will this person like the kind of work we have and/or can he or she handle a lot of responsibility?

You can see the challenge in this question. Going on too long will only make the interviewer think you have a problem in getting things done or being cooperative. You might share a story where you were involved in a project that was not completed. After your part was done and the work was handed off to another area, it was made a low priority on their things to do list, and was never completed. It was difficult not to see success achieved.

N. Explain why you attended the college you selected.
Possible Meaning: Did this person have a plan when selecting a college?

While the best answer is probably because they have a great business program and you wanted a degree in business, I believe many answers will work here. For instance, I worked while attending college and paid for it on my own and this was the one that was most affordable. Here you've gotten out the fact that you are a hard worker and you did what you had to do to get your education. Or, I was a collegiate athlete and I felt this university had the best combination of coaches and academic professors. Or, the school has a focus on communications which was a weakness of mine I wanted to improve on since I believe it's key to success in business. I hope you agree these are all decent responses. Just make sure you stay away from responses that put you at the bottom of the candidate list such as, all my friends went there, my best friend decided to attend, my father or mother went to this university, or I didn't want to stay at home. These latter responses only serve to make you look like you don't make your own decisions and/or have had no real direction or goals in your life.

O. State leisure activities, which provide the most satisfaction.
Possible Meaning: Are you an active person with a lot of energy or more of an introvert? Will your personality fit well in our organization?

If asked feel free to share whatever it is you like as long as it's clean, wholesome fun; such as fishing, biking, walking, tennis, golf, knitting, boating, reading, softball, or whatever. Just make sure you have at least two or three things here since again, saying nothing or barely something, could work against you. Employers want energetic hard-working people that enjoy life (translation—have a very positive attitude) and are aware of what's going on in the world. On the flip side, don't over do it by saying that you go boating every weekend or play tennis three times or more a week. This can make an employer concerned you won't be available or unwilling to put in some extra time when a big job calls for it.

P. Explain things that you and your last supervisor disagreed on.
Possible Meaning: This probably most of the time translates into "what didn't you like about your last supervisor?"

Be careful with this question since your answer really shows if you got along well with management. Pick something that in the big scheme of things was minor. This is an area in which you really want to start off on the right foot. An example I used at times was that my latest boss used to love giving individual praise and awards in team meetings. While I've got nothing against individual praise and awards I think it conflicts with truly supporting team efforts. I believe individual praise and awards should be given individually and the only team awards in front of the whole team. Just a personal belief that I'm sure many companies would not agree with. I'm sure you'll have no trouble finding other inconsequential areas of disagreement. Note, that you should have a couple of these for several of your past supervisors, not just the latest.

Q. Describe your last supervisor's greatest strengths.
Possible Meaning: What traits and strengths do you admire in a manager or management team?

This is one of the easier questions assuming it is easy for you to pick out some of the good quality strengths of previous supervisors. Don't get too carried away and list or describe too many making your self look like an overly optimistic and possibly unrealistic person. You should also make sure you don't provide strengths that are too minor such as, fair, honest, hard working. These don't have quite enough bite for this question and make you appear shallow or unable to evaluate another person's strengths and weaknesses, which is a skill you may need especially if interviewing for a management position. While you can use some of the more shallow items I've given you above, you most definitely want to include strengths that promote skills and abilities important in doing a quality job. For instance, detail mindedness, thoroughness, goal oriented, and extremely dedicated and professional are good. Be ready with examples to support how your last supervisor exhibited these strengths.

R. Describe areas you felt your supervisor could have done a better job.
Possible Meaning: What types of things frustrate you and what qualities do you like in a manager?

I like to keep the focus here on items someone in management can control. For instance, something like better communication regarding department actions and plans. This simply lets the interviewer know you like to be involved with what is going on and if the interviewer is your prospective boss, they know they can control this issue. Contrast this with possibly saying you wish your last supervisor would have more consistently achieved objectives. What if actually completing objectives in this new operation are contingent on many factors? You've just planted a seed in this employer's mind that you may become frustrated if he or she doesn't achieve goals and they could be out of their control. Not good.

S. Explain how your last supervisor treated you.
Possible Meaning: Do you consider yourself having ever been mistreated by a boss?

Not a question you want to be negative with at all. Never give anyone the impression that problems you have confronted were someone else's fault. Even if they were, stick to a solid and brief response. My last supervisor was tough, demanding, but fair.

T. Describe ways in which your supervisor developed your skills.
Possible Meaning: Do you want to learn and/or are you interested in professional growth?

Share stories about educational opportunities past employers have supported and you have participated in. It would be wise to bring up those situations in which you completed the requirements for a designation or certification.

Another angle is to share information regarding projects and tasks you were assigned and allowed to manage from beginning to end with little supervision or assistance from your supervisor. Your supervisor allowed you to make mistakes, learn, and develop your skills.

U. Describe the type of supervisor you feel you work best for.
Possible Meaning: Do the traits you'd like in a boss match with the manager of this position?

I like to answer this with sharing that I like a boss that is progressive minded, open, and willing to try new things; one that truly allows employees to contribute to the company's success. I think this response says that you are a very self-motivated hardworking person. If this is the truth and you are a real go-getter, and freedom in your work is important to you, than this is a good response. If not, you may want to respond differently to this question and/or tone down what I've suggested.

V. Describe the job duties, which gave you the most satisfaction.
Possible Meaning: What does this person really like to do? Do the responsibilities of the position truly match the candidate's interests?

My response to this question is making improvements. To see the operation improve, to get better results, to see a team come together, that is all the reward I need. While this is a generic response and you could be pressed to provide some specifics, I've not provided anything in my statement that wouldn't match up with the job responsibilities. I've left myself open as a candidate that might fit. If you are pressed for details, try to maintain a generic approach. Try something like, I enjoyed organizing the work, as the heavy workload was very challenging to maintain. You can only hope organizational skills are a key requirement for the job. If prior to this interview you have knowledge of some of the job responsibilities I highly recommend using those duties you liked most that tie in with the responsibilities of the position in order to put your best foot forward.

W. Describe the job duties, which gave you the least satisfaction.
Possible Meaning: How much can this candidate handle?

Be careful not to run on here since this can only serve to make you look as someone who could get down and negative about your work. I've used disciplining employees who decided not to commit to the team. This to me was a distraction from our efforts to achieve our goals and unfortunate that we did not establish mutual interest and dedication with this particular team member. I think this example shows the employer I take employee development seriously and focuses on a personnel problem, which is not directly related to the work. I can support the latter by sharing that I enjoy my work citing examples of awards and/or complimentary letters my team received. Keep in mind that it is probably unwise to say there is nothing you don't like. So have a few of your least favorites ready to go, and limit your discussion to what you think fits best.

X. Explain the progress you have made with your present company.
Possible Meaning: Does this candidate take on more responsibility if asked? Does he or she take initiative and pride in succeeding?

Be ready with internal move and promotion data. If you have not moved up within your present organization, than share specific accomplishments made and/or additional responsibilities accepted in your present position. No matter how you specifically answer this question, once again, and I know I'm starting to sound like a broken record, keep it positive. If you paint a picture that you became unsatisfied with a past employer the prospective employer is only going to wonder why you have remained employed with them. If you're lucky you can use a reason like the last I was able to. I was working for a small employer that ran into financial problems and began laying off staff. Growth opportunities were limited.

Y. Explain what you expect out of a job.
Possible Meaning: Does this candidate's overall job requirements match what we are trying to accomplish?

I'd suggest remaining generic with this question stating something like challenge and opportunity for growth. It is important not to knock yourself out of contention by providing unrealistic expectations or expectations so removed from the position the employer immediately realizes this is not a match.

Z. Explain what you expect from the company who hires you.
Possible Meaning: Do expectations here match what the candidate has indicated are their strengths and what they've said they can do for the organization?

As you may have noticed, some of these questions (and possible meanings) most definitely begin to run together and some even are repetitive. Understand, that many employers ask questions to see if the candidate is consistent in their responses. For instance, we could answer this question very similarly to others already on this list. I like to go with simply stating that I'd like to work for an organization that takes pride in what they do and looks to be either a leader or one of the best in their industry.

AA. Relay how long you been searching for this type of job.
Possible Meaning: Has this candidate been looking for a while and is there some reason or reasons they have not secured a position earlier?

The best response to this question, if you remain gainfully employed at the time, is to say that in the past two weeks you have become serious about your job search. Even if you've been looking for quite some time this is your best answer. However, if you have been laid off, you should always share the complete truth to this question and provide the amount of time you have been looking. Leave it at that and do not try to provide any reasons for your delay in landing a job, unless the reason(s) is that you have received several offers but you did not believe the position(s) would offer the challenge you need in your work.

AB. Describe your outstanding qualities.
Possible Meaning: Does the candidate have a lack of confidence, confidence, or arrogance? Do outstanding qualities match with strengths and interests?

Again, this is a question we've really seen already. This should tie in directly with your strengths and you should make very sure you are consistent. If asked this as well as what are your strengths, take the opportunity without going overboard to brag about your qualities and show them how you can add value! Some I like to use are energy, attitude, persistency, and organizational skills.

AC. Describe areas you feel you need improvement.
Possible Meaning: Is the candidate honest? Does the candidate have weaknesses that would make it difficult for them to succeed in this position?

This is a tricky question simply because you don't want to make yourself look too bad, however saying nothing can make you look too confident or even arrogant. I like to go with patience and/or computer skills—like learning more about Excel, Word, etcetera. I think patience is fine, since it implies you like to get things done—which is what most employers really want in an employee. Using computer skills can be dangerous if the job requires advanced skills in these areas. Hopefully you acquired some knowledge about the position and can come up with areas needing improvement that you can learn while on the job.

AD. Explain why you would like to work for their company.
Possible Meaning: Does the answer to this question flow with the answer to why the candidate has come to our organization?

If you've done any research you might simply state that you know this organization is growing and you want to be a part of and contribute to success now and in the future. Keep in mind that even very little research will allow you to make such statements. For instance, if in your job search you simply found a list of the fastest growing companies in your city, you just qualified yourself to make the statement above. Whatever you do, keep it simple and stay consistent with responses you gave to similar questions. Do you recall that for the initial question of why you have come to them, I suggested saying that they are growing and/or because they have a good reputation and you would like to remain in your community. If you used growing earlier we're in good shape with our response to this question. If you used good reputation and a desire to remain in your community, the best response here is say the same and add that you also have an understanding they are growing and that is exciting!

AE. Describe what you think determines an employee's progress in a company.
Possible Meaning: Can this candidate handle a very direct question in an appropriate manner and are they always focused on getting results?

Stay direct and simple in your answer to this question. I believe the best answer is achievement of desired results, positive effect on others, and consistently adding value to the organization. In other words, your work is improving the company. I once read an article that said all improvements to an organization fall into four categories; Revenue Enhancement, Improved Quality, Customer Goodwill, and Expense Reduction. If asked to really specify what you've done or think you need to do to succeed, make sure it falls under one of these categories.

AF. Describe a situation when you organized a project.
Possible Meaning: Has this candidate truly coordinated any projects? Were the projects completed? Were the projects of a substantive nature?

If you haven't organized any, say you haven't. It is very likely if you misrepresent yourself in this matter, the prospective employer will find out. And while we're touching of the subject of honesty, I personally vote for complete honesty 100% of the time. Make and keep your career and life on track and allow yourself to sleep easy at night knowing you do the right thing. If you have coordinated some key projects, then relay what you have done, why it was important to the company, and the results you achieved. As usual, don't go on to long. Show this employer you can communicate in a brief and effective manner.

AG. Describe a situation when you disciplined an employee.
Possible Meaning: Is this candidate capable of showing compassion coupled with the fortitude to handle tough tasks and get the job done?

Once again, if you haven't managed anyone and this is the first management position you are going for, than speak the truth. Let's assume you have managed and are attempting to land another or higher-level management role. In the latter case simply describe a situation explaining why you had to discipline the employee, what steps you took to discipline, and the result. Keep it short and share how difficult it was as disciplining is never an easy task. This allows the employer to see your compassionate side, which is important in building an effective team.

AH. Describe a time when you handled a difficult situation.
Possible Meaning: What is difficult to this candidate? Will this candidate meet with the same kind of challenges in our position?

I like to use the same answer I used in question AH. My reasoning is that disciplining is very time consuming and difficult to complete while you try to remain effective in getting the job done day to day. Additionally, if this is your most difficult situation I think it bodes well for you that it's pretty easy for you to get the job done. The danger here is that the interviewer may request another example and once again you need to be prepared. You might use the loss of a key employee as an example sharing that he or she was very instrumental in the department achieving our objectives and it took time and diligence to get her replacement up to speed.

IMPORTANT NOTE:

Many companies use questions that start with "Describe for me…a time…a situation…a challenge" which force the candidate to come up with real life occurrences in order to answer the question. While I gave you a few samples at the end of my list, you should be prepared for this type of questioning as it can unnerve many candidates. One of the best ways to be prepared is to review your resume' in complete detail and make a list citing personal stories that support <u>everything</u> on your resume'. That's right, <u>everything</u>!

4. **QUESTIONS TO ASK IN INTERVIEWS**

(NOTE: Questions are broken down by who is your audience and within that, by categories; Company, Department, Position, Boss, Peers, and Staff.)

QUESTIONS FOR PERSONNEL:
- A. COMPANY
  - I. Can I have an organizational chart to visualize the company structure?
  - II. What is the size of the company; number of employees, net income?
  - III. What is the company's growth rate over the last 5 years?
  - IV. What are other job openings presently available in the company?
  - V. What do you believe are the future opportunities in this organization?

- B. DEPARTMENT
  - I. Why was this department created?
  - II. What purpose does this department serve?
  - III. How long has the department been in existence?
  - IV. Can you sum up the objective of the department?
  - V. Are there any time bombs confronting the department?

- C. POSITION
  - I. Is this position open as a result of growth or a replacement?
  - II. If growth, is it a new position or has someone been promoted?
  - III. Is someone else performing the same type of work done in this position?
  - IV. If someone is being replaced, is that person still with the company?
  - V. Can I meet with the person who previously held this position?
  - VI. If position open due to promotion, why was the incumbent promoted?
  - VII. What do you believe is the least appealing aspect of the job?

VIII. What do you believe are the biggest opportunities in this position?

IX. What do you believe are the most difficult problems this person would face?

D. BOSS

I. What is the boss' background?

II. Could you describe the boss' style?

III. How long has the boss been with the organization?

IV. How long has the boss been in the business?

E. PEERS

I. Anyone within the company being considered for the position?

II. Can you describe the last person who held this job?

F. STAFF (If going for a management position.)

I. General or overall qualifications?

II. Experience levels?

III. Average tenure?

IV. What is turnover rate?

V. Do you believe compensation is accurate for the job and area?

VI. What is your confidence in finding good employees in this area?

QUESTIONS FOR PEERS OR LAST PERSON WHO HELD POSITION:

A. COMPANY

I. What is the company's image in people's minds?

II. What are people's attitudes towards company?

III. Is the company open to change?

IV. What do you believe are the future opportunities in this organization?

B. DEPARTMENT

I. Can you sum up the objective of the department?

    II. Are there any time bombs confronting the department?
C. POSITION
    I. What is the least appealing aspect of the job?
    II. What are the biggest opportunities?
    III. What are the most difficult problems you faced?
    IV. What do you think is the biggest challenge of this position right now?
    V. What opportunities are there to learn?
D. BOSS
    I. Is the prospective boss as charming as he/she appears?
    II. Can you briefly describe the person I would report to?
    III. Can you describe the bosses' management style?
    IV. How long has the boss been in the business?
    V. How long has the boss been with the company?
    VI. What is the bosses' background?
E. PEERS
    I. Anyone within the company being considered for the position?
    II. Can you describe the last person who held this job?
F. STAFF (If going for a management position.)
    I. General or overall qualifications?
    II. Experience levels?
    III. Average tenure?
    IV. Do you believe compensation is accurate for the job and area?

QUESTIONS FOR PROSPECTIVE BOSS:
A. COMPANY
    I. Does company maintain internal promoting policy?
    II. Any time bombs confronting company?
    III. Where is growth coming from?

- IV. Who are the major competitors?
- V. What is the company's major source of income?
- VI. How do we stack up against competition? Do we benchmark?
- VII. Does the company have a mission statement?
- VIII. Does the company have a vision or picture of the future?
- IX. Can you give me a picture of today versus the future in terms of
  a. Revenue, b. Profit, c. Number of employees, d. Overall growth
- X. What is the image of the company in people's minds?
- XI. What are people's attitudes towards the company?
- XII. How long has the CEO been with the company?
- XIII. What is the present size of company in terms of
  a. Number of employees, b. Revenue, c. Net income, d. Market share
- XIV. How does the company help individuals & departments meet goals?
  a. Computer systems? b. Telecommunications? c. Etcetera?
- XV. What is company turnover rate?
- XVI. What are present products and/or services offered by company?

B. DEPARTMENT
- I. Why was this department created?
- II. What purpose does this department serve?
- III. How long has the department been in existence?
- IV. Can you sum up the objective of the department?
- V. Are there any time bombs confronting the department?
- VI. How critical are the results of this unit to the success of the company?
- VII. What kind of MIS support is in place?
- VIII. What kinds of relationship(s) exist between MIS and this department?
- IX. What is average tenure of MIS staff?

X. How experienced is the MIS staff with the department processes?

C. POSITION
  I. What are the major job responsibilities?
  II. Can you describe the activities of a typical day?
  III. What do you see as the toughest challenge in this job?
  IV. What has been position turnover in the last five years?
  V. Are there any technical requirements for the position?
  VI. What type of training programs are available and supported by the company?

D. BOSS
  I. Could you elaborate on your background; Education? Career?
  II. How do you measure performance?
  III. How would you describe yourself as a manager?
  IV. Are you more hands on or hands off? Can you give me some examples?
  V. Can you tell me what the last person you hired did well and not well?
  VI. What should someone who works for you do best in order to succeed?
  VII. What should someone who works for you never do?
  VIII. What are some of the ideas you presently have to improve the operation?
  IX. Who makes the systems development decisions; software and hardware?
  X. Could you pick a metaphor, such as an orchestra conductor or football coach or army sergeant, that best captures the way you like to work with subordinates?

E. PEERS
  I. Anyone in the organization being considered for the position?
  II. Can you describe the last person you hired?

F. STAFF (If going for a management position.)
  I. General or overall qualifications?
  II. Experience levels?
  III. Average tenure?
  IV. What is turnover rate?
  V. Do you believe compensation is accurate for the job and area?
  VI. What is your confidence in finding good employees in this area?

QUESTIONS IF RELOCATION IS INVOLVED:
A. Does the company cover the costs and provide temporary living accommodations?
B. Does the company cover the costs of any:
  I. Legal fees
  II. Real estate commissions
  III. House hunting trips
  IV. Incidental moving costs
C. Does the company help a spouse find employment?

INFORMATION YOU SHOULD GATHER IF RELOCATION IS INVOLVED:
A. Determine the quality of school systems.
B. Determine housing costs.
C. Determine housing availability.
D. Determine the cost of living in the area.
E. Determine the quality of state park systems.
F. Determine the availability of shopping facilities.
G. Determine the cultural activities available.
H. Determine the states crime rate.

RATIONALE:

Asking questions is a key element of the successful interview and allows you to truly find out if the organization, position, and boss are a good match for you. You should view all interviews as 50/50, meaning you are interviewing them as much as they are interviewing you!

IMPORTANT NOTE:

As you've noticed there are many questions in this area. You will very likely not be able to nor should you try to ask all of them. You should read these "questions to ask" very carefully and select those you believe are important to you. Additionally, if the company requires you to go through numerous interviews and/or seems very open to answering questions, you should proceed with asking more! And finally, keep in mind this listing is in no specific sequence. You will most likely want to re-arrange the order in which you ask some of these questions, again, based on your situation.

STEP 3
BEGIN TO APPROACH THE JOB MARKET

THERE ARE 3 WAYS TO APPROACH THE JOB MARKET:

1. **NETWORKING**

    A. Employer Contacts

    B. Personal Contacts

2. **ISSUING RESUMES'**

    A. Newspaper advertisements

    B. Online sources

3. **SEARCH FIRM CONTACTS**

1. **NETWORKING**

    A. **Employer Contacts**

    I. Create a list of the top twenty five companies you'd like to work for. Use a local business journal or publication to create this list.

    II. Complete a network contact report for each company. (See pages 36-37.)

    III. Mail networking letters to each of your companies. (See pages 38-39.)

    IV. Five to six days later call each of your companies. (See page 40.)

    V. Meet and get advice from your contacts. (See pages 41-42.)

    VI. After <u>every</u> phone call and <u>every</u> meeting, immediately log all information on your network contact report!

    VII. Always send a thank you note. (See pages 43-44.)

    VIII. If someone's advice was fruitful, send another thank you follow up letter. (See pages 45-46.)

    IX. Mail letters to companies you would like to work for, to persons with power to hire you asking for an interview and follow up with a call. This is not a networking letter! (See pages 47-48.)

    B. **Personal Contacts**

    I. Create a list of twenty five of your best personal contacts.

    II. Follow the same procedures as outlined above for employer contacts.

NETWORK CONTACT REPORT

NAME: _____

TITLE: _____

COMPANY: _____

ADDRESS: _____

_____

CITY, STATE, ZIP: _____

PHONE: _____

CALL/LETTER DOCUMENTATION:
(Dates/Topics)

_____
_____
_____
_____
_____
_____
_____
_____
_____
_____
_____
_____
_____
_____
_____
_____
_____

NETWORK CONTACT REPORT

RATIONALE:

As you begin this system of job hunting it quickly becomes apparent that it is impossible to remember and keep organized all the individual's names, company's names, addresses, phone numbers, conversations, meeting dates, directions, and more that you will accumulate, without logging this information. The networking contact report enables you to remain highly organized and even impress some employers in your ability to recall details of conversations held weeks earlier!

NETWORK LETTER TO YOUR COMPANIES
1st LETTER

TODAY'S DATE

NEW COMPANY NAME
ATTN: NEW COMPANY CONTACT NAME
NEW COMPANY STREET ADDRESS
NEW COMPANY CITY, STATE, AND ZIP

Dear PERSON WITH THE POWER TO HIRE:

My expertise is in (FIELD OF EXPERTISE). I'm very good at what I do!

During my (NUMBER OF YEARS IN YOUR PROFESSION) year career I have faced numerous difficult and challenging situations. I overcame obstacles by implementing a sound business strategy focused on basic management principles and am able to quickly contribute to a company's success.

While presently happy and reasonably challenged, my ultimate objective is to obtain a (TITLE OF POSITION YOU DESIRE) position. To that end, if you could direct me to anyone in your organization possibly looking for someone with my experience and skills, or provide any advice as to the direction I might take or suggest anyone in the industry I might talk to regarding positions in my area of interest, it would be greatly appreciated.

While I'm sure you are very busy I'd like to take you out for a quick lunch to ask a few questions and promise we can be as brief as you like. I will follow-up with a call to set up a time that is the most convenient for you.

If you would like to speak with me prior, don't hesitate to call.

Sincerely,

YOUR TYPED NAME
YOUR STREET ADDRESS
YOUR CITY, STATE, AND ZIP
YOUR HOME AREA CODE AND PHONE NUMBER
YOUR WORK AREA CODE AND PHONE NUMBER
YOUR CELL AREA CODE AND PHONE NUMBER

NETWORK LETTER TO YOUR COMPANIES
1st LETTER

RATIONALE:

Your first contact should be made through the mail if for nothing else, because it will give you a reason for calling. The letter is a way to simply ask for assistance and advice. Keep it friendly and inquisitive in nature while throwing in a little bit about your background, experiences, and successes.

NETWORK FOLLOWUP CALL GUIDELINES

Mr./Mrs. _____,

I'm calling in regards to the letter I sent several days ago.

I simply:

1. Wanted to make sure you received my letter.
2. Wanted to see if we could meet briefly for lunch, or before or after work, and you'd be kind enough to allow me to ask a few questions that may assist me in my job search. Lunch would be on me!
3. Promise our meeting will be as short as you like and would appreciate any information you could share.
4. I also wanted to ask if you know of anyone or any organization that may be interested in someone with my background?
5. IMPORTANT NOTE:
   If you receive any hesitancy or question regarding why they should meet with you simply say you are interested in what they have to say about the industry, the job market, and your approach and resume'. You would really appreciate their advice!

RATIONALE:

It is important to contact the prospective employer and get a face-to-face meeting where you can display your personality, inquisitive nature, and most importantly, your determination to find a position in a firm where you can solidly contribute to the success of the organization.

NETWORK MEETING GUIDELINES

1. Thank them for taking time from their busy schedule to meet with you.
2. Ask the following series of questions in your networking meeting:
    a. Have you had an opportunity to review my resume'?
    b. What do you think of my resume'?
    c. Could you give me a few general opinions?
    d. If your or an employer like yours received it, how do you think they'd react?
    e. What do you see as potential strengths and/or weaknesses of the resume'?
    f. What would you recommend as the best approach for this industry?
    g. I've targeted these companies, would you recommend any others?
    h. What do you think of my overall campaign approach?
    i. How did you get started in this line of work?
    j. What do you like best about your job?
    k. What do you like best about the industry?
    l. What do you like least about your job?
    m. What do you like least about the industry?
    n. What do you believe is the major reason for your success?
    o. What are the biggest challenges you presently face?
    p. What do you think of opportunities in this industry at this time?
    q. Do you know of any companies doing well in this business?
    r. Do you know of anyone working at some of the companies I've targeted?
    s. Would you recommend anyone I could speak with at these companies?
    t. Are you aware of any other companies, which could use my skills?
    u. If you hear of any opportunities within your organization or others, would you please keep me in mind?

IMPORTANT NOTE:
You will most likely not be able to or want to ask all of these questions. Therefore, focus on the ones most important to you.

3. Never ask for a job, always ask for suggestions!
4. Don't ask for favors; always ask for advice!
5. Take resumes' along, but don't offer unless asked.
6. Deliver a brief background summary to include why you want to leave your present company/position and describe the type of position you want.
7. Leave a resume' behind if the individual seems receptive.

RATIONALE:

It is important to let the contact see just how good you are in person; personality, dedication, determination, etcetera! Additionally, this meeting should be equally focused on obtaining other contacts and information that will assist you in your job search.

NETWORK THANK YOU LETTER

TODAY'S DATE

NEW COMPANY NAME
ATTN: NEW COMPANY CONTACT NAME
NEW COMPANY STREET ADDRESS
NEW COMPANY CITY, STATE, AND ZIP

Dear PERSON WITH THE POWER TO HIRE:

This is just a note to thank you for taking time from your busy schedule to meet with me.

Your advice is highly appreciated and I plan on quickly putting it to use.

I believe the information and suggestions you provided will be very beneficial.

If I can ever be of any assistance to you, please do not hesitate to call.

Sincerely,

YOUR TYPED NAME
YOUR STREET ADDRESS
YOUR CITY, STATE, AND ZIP
YOUR HOME AREA CODE AND PHONE NUMBER
YOUR WORK AREA CODE AND PHONE NUMBER

RATIONALE:

It is important to thank anyone that gave you some of his or her time. It is also important to show that you are considerate. And lastly, you should take every opportunity possible to put your name in front of them.

NETWORK FOLLOW-UP LETTER

TODAY'S DATE

NEW COMPANY NAME
ATTN: NEW COMPANY CONTACT NAME
NEW COMPANY STREET ADDRESS
NEW COMPANY CITY, STATE, AND ZIP

Dear PERSON WITH THE POWER TO HIRE:

We met some time ago, I believe on (DAY OF THE WEEK, MONTH, DATE). At that meeting you provided me with the advice I contact (NAME OF CONTACT) in regards to my job campaign.

Your advice has proven fruitful and I have sent this short note just to say thank you. I will never forget your help.

If I can ever be of any assistance, do not hesitate to call.

Sincerely,

YOUR TYPED NAME
YOUR STREET ADDRESS
YOUR CITY, STATE, AND ZIP
YOUR HOME AREA CODE AND PHONE NUMBER
YOUR WORK AREA CODE AND PHONE NUMBER

RATIONALE:

Often this letter is unnecessary, as you have already generated enough activity to keep you very busy, and/or even landed a position. However, in the event you are still looking for employment, this letter can be helpful. Again the idea is to thank your initial contact for their assistance and simply get your name in front of them once again.

NETWORK INTERVIEW REQUEST LETTER

TODAY'S DATE

NEW COMPANY NAME
ATTN: NEW COMPANY CONTACT NAME
NEW COMPANY STREET ADDRESS
NEW COMPANY CITY, STATE, AND ZIP

Dear PERSON WITH THE POWER TO HIRE:

We met several months ago and briefly discussed our industry and career interests. You provided me with some valuable advice at that time. I wanted to first thank you again for that information.

While I am reasonably challenged in my present position, it is unlikely I'll be able to achieve the position I truly desire as a result of (STATE COMPANY'S REASON FOR NO GROWTH OPPORTUNITIES).

Consequently, the time is right to ask if (NEW COMPANY NAME) might have a place for an exceptional "progressive minded" team member.

To refresh your memory, my expertise is in (STATE AREA OF EXPERTISE). I am very good at what I do and my track record demonstrates my advanced skills. I have achieved numerous accomplishments in several different environments.

I will call you next week and expand on this letter. Do not hesitate to call if you would like to speak with me prior to that time.

Sincerely,

YOUR TYPED NAME
YOUR STREET ADDRESS
YOUR CITY, STATE, AND ZIP
YOUR HOME AREA CODE AND PHONE NUMBER
YOUR WORK AREA CODE AND PHONE NUMBER

RATIONALE:

Often this letter is unnecessary, as you have already generated enough activity and landed the position you wanted. However, if you are still seeking employment, it is time to ask your networking contacts for an interview. Again, thank them for all their assistance up until this point, but push to see if you can meet with them or someone in the organization in order to interview for any possible openings that fit your interests and qualifications.

2. **ISSUING RESUMES'**

   A. **Newspaper advertisements**

   I. Send your resume responding to advertisements for jobs that match your background. Do not rely on this method and continue to focus on earlier networking activities as planned.

   To enhance the low probability of generating activity from newspaper advertisements one action to take is altering your resume' to include the same wording used in the advertisement. This can only help to increase your chances of obtaining an interview.

   B. **Online sources**

   I. After completion of your resume', post it on some online sites, to include: monster.com, jobs.com, hotjobs.com, nationjob.com, careerbuilder.com, flipdog.com, jobsonline.com, headhunter.com, and jobsniper.com. But don't expect much from this method! There are millions of job hunters that use this method. Your chances of getting noticed and/or creating much activity from this method are very limited. While some employers use this method effectively, most do not. Your best way of creating opportunities for yourself is by selecting companies you would like to work for, networking, and creating face-to-face meetings, all of which we've discussed earlier.

ISSUING RESUMES' EMPLOYER DIRECT LETTER

TODAY'S DATE

NEW COMPANY NAME
ATTN: NEW COMPANY CONTACT NAME
NEW COMPANY STREET ADDRESS
NEW COMPANY CITY, STATE, AND ZIP

Dear PERSON WITH THE POWER TO HIRE:

Early in my career I learned what it takes to increase revenues and decrease costs. During my (NUMBER OF YEARS IN YOUR PROFESSION) year career I have faced numerous difficult and challenging situations. I overcame obstacles by implementing a sound strategy focused on basic management principles.

The enclosed resume highlights my experience in (YOUR JOB TITLE AND/OR EXPERIENCES) and demonstrates my exceptional motivational, administrative, and organization skills. By utilizing these skills I have been able to achieve numerous accomplishments in several different environments. I would imagine your firm would be most interested in my background.

I would like to further discuss the (EXACT TITLE OF POSITION BEING SOUGHT) position opening.

Feel free to contact me at either work or home. Thank you for your consideration.

Sincerely,

YOUR TYPED NAME
YOUR STREET ADDRESS
YOUR CITY, STATE, AND ZIP
YOUR HOME AREA CODE AND PHONE NUMBER
YOUR WORK AREA CODE AND PHONE NUMBER

ISSUING RESUMES' INTERVIEW FOLLOW-UP

TODAY'S DATE

NEW COMPANY NAME
ATTN: NEW COMPANY CONTACT NAME
NEW COMPANY STREET ADDRESS
NEW COMPANY CITY, STATE, AND ZIP

Dear PERSON WITH THE POWER TO HIRE:

I wanted to thank you for the opportunity to discuss the (EXACT TITLE OF POSITION BEING SOUGHT) position opening at (NEW COMPANY NAME).

I hope that after our discussion, it is readily apparent I am motivated and qualified. I am very much interested in the position and would appreciate your careful evaluation of my credentials and experience.

If I can be of any assistance in your evaluation of my qualifications, please let me know. I can be reached at either my work or home.

Sincerely,

YOUR TYPED NAME
YOUR STREET ADDRESS
YOUR CITY, STATE, AND ZIP
YOUR HOME AREA CODE AND PHONE NUMBER
YOUR WORK AREA CODE AND PHONE NUMBER

ISSUING RESUMES' APPLICATION FOLLOW-UP

TODAY'S DATE

NEW COMPANY NAME
ATTN: NEW COMPANY CONTACT NAME
NEW COMPANY STREET ADDRESS
NEW COMPANY CITY, STATE, AND ZIP

Dear PERSON WITH THE POWER TO HIRE:

I have enclosed an application regarding the (EXACT TITLE OF POSITION BEING SOUGHT) position opening. Should you have any further questions, feel free to contact me.

I appreciated the opportunity to discuss the position with you.

I look forward to the opportunity of joining (NEW COMPANY NAME).

Sincerely,

YOUR TYPED NAME
YOUR STREET ADDRESS
YOUR CITY, STATE, AND ZIP
YOUR HOME AREA CODE AND PHONE NUMBER
YOUR WORK AREA CODE AND PHONE NUMBER

ISSUING RESUMES' CALL FOLLOW-UP

TODAY'S DATE

NEW COMPANY NAME
ATTN: NEW COMPANY CONTACT NAME
NEW COMPANY STREET ADDRESS
NEW COMPANY CITY, STATE, AND ZIP

Dear PERSON WITH THE POWER TO HIRE:

Thanks for your return call on (DAY OF THE WEEK, MONTH, DATE, AND YEAR). I was pleased to learn that I am still being considered for the (EXACT TITLE OF POSITION BEING SOUGHT) position.

I was impressed with everyone's presentation of the company, the professionalism, and the company's facility.

I sincerely hope mutual interest is achieved. Should you have any further questions, please feel free to call me.

Sincerely,

YOUR TYPED NAME
YOUR STREET ADDRESS
YOUR CITY, STATE, AND ZIP
YOUR HOME AREA CODE AND PHONE NUMBER
YOUR WORK AREA CODE AND PHONE NUMBER

ISSUING RESUMES' DELAY FOLLOW-UP

TODAY'S DATE

NEW COMPANY NAME
ATTN: NEW COMPANY CONTACT NAME
NEW COMPANY STREET ADDRESS
NEW COMPANY CITY, STATE, AND ZIP

Dear PERSON WITH THE POWER TO HIRE:

Although it has been quite some time since our initial meeting, it is my understanding I am still being considered for the (EXACT TITLE OF POSITION BEING SOUGHT) position. I was extremely pleased to learn this. I am still interested and simply wanted to express that interest.

If you should have any questions during further review of my qualifications, do not hesitate to call me.

Sincerely,

YOUR TYPED NAME
YOUR STREET ADDRESS
YOUR CITY, STATE, AND ZIP
YOUR HOME AREA CODE AND PHONE NUMBER
YOUR WORK AREA CODE AND PHONE NUMBER

3. SEARCH FIRM CONTACTS

Contact several, I recommend no more than three, search firms in your area and obtain their assistance with your search. Research these firms prior to doing any business with them and ensure they are reputable. Also, make sure that these firms do not charge any fees. Regardless of what "they" say, you should not have to pay to find a job and/or get hired. Quality employers will pay the fees to these firms in order to find quality employees.

SEARCH FIRM CONTACT CALL GUIDELINES

Make calls to search firms and interview them to find out if they can assist you in your job search. Ask them the following questions;

1. Do you work with people in the _____ (your industry)?
2. Do you work with people in clerical, supervisory, management, and/or executive level positions?
3. Are you able to take on additional assignments at this time?
4. Do you charge for your services?

IMPORTANT NOTE:

You should not have to pay for <u>any</u> services. Good companies will pay the search firm for finding good employees.

SEARCH FIRM CONTACT FOLLOW-UP LETTER

TODAY'S DATE

SEARCH FIRM NAME
ATTN: SEARCH FIRM CONTACT NAME
SEARCH FIRM STREET ADDRESS
SEARCH FIRM CITY, STATE, AND ZIP

Dear SEARCH FIRM CONTACT:

Per our conversation, I have enclosed my resume for your review. In addition, I would like to tell you a little about myself:

I am mainly interested in (NAME(S) OF POSITIONS YOU DESIRE) positions. I would consider a change in career fields and industries. Other areas of interest in which I believe I am capable of making a substantive contribution include (OTHER FIELDS YOU CAN ADAPT TO AND WOULD LIKE).

I am a (LIST YOUR STRONG QUALITIES) professional.

I am only interested in employer contingency agreements.

I have not been interviewing with other firms as I am gainfully employed. At this time I am looking to establish several contacts that will apprise me of any opportunities that arise in which my skills can be utilized. I am an extremely ambitious individual.

While I am aware all exchanges of information between us will be held in strict confidence, please make sure my present employer, (STATE NAME), is not contacted.

If the right opportunity should arise, please contact me at either work or home. Should you have any questions regarding the enclosed resume or the aforementioned information, again feel free to contact me.

Sincerely,

YOUR TYPED NAME
YOUR STREET ADDRESS
YOUR CITY, STATE, AND ZIP
YOUR HOME AREA CODE AND PHONE NUMBER
YOUR WORK AREA CODE AND PHONE NUMBER

PPLA, Inc.
JOB HUNTING SERVICES APPLICATION

OPTION	OPTION DESCRIPTION	OPTION COST
A	A professionally written resume'.	_____$100.00
B	A professionally written resume' and feedback and guidance on interviewing question preparation. (Three months.)	_____$125.00
C	A professionally written resume', feedback and guidance on interviewing question preparation, and assistance during implementation of methods to approach the job market. (Three months.)	_____$150.00

To purchase any of our job search services visit our website at **PPLAservicesforyou.com**, print off a copy of this form that you will find on our website, write an "X" on the pertinent line above indicating your choice, and sign and date the form as requested. NOTE; when you print off this form, you'll also get the rest of the required application.

Complete the application in it's entirety and mail it and & your payment to
PPLA, Inc.
2675 Kettering CT.
St. Charles, MO 63303

Make checks payable to; Griff Stevens c/o PPLA, Inc.
At this time we accept checks only.
If you have questions contact us at: **636-477-8801; Mon–Fri;** 7 AM-4 PM.

EPILOGUE

An underlying trait that all successful job hunters must possess is a strong and very positive attitude. Job hunters must look past rejection, remained focused on their goals, and not allow themselves to become unnerved at the barrage of questions and situations they will confront.

To that end, my epilogue is simply a true story, my true story, which solidified in me a very strong positive attitude for the rest of my life.

While I had normally always been a very strong, very hard working, energetic person, in 1995 a few incidents in my life made me question my worth and the worth of others. What I now consider a small miracle took place in that same year and made me realize we can accomplish anything we set our minds to and that others will help you get there.

If you take the time to read my story, I hope that it inspires you as it has me, to live every aspect of your life to the fullest. And unlike me, maybe you can start living your life to the fullest without having to wait for a miracle.

The Signs & An Angel

As I woke each morning feelings of loneliness and failure would overwhelm me and unfortunately linger in my mind throughout each day. Nineteen ninety-five had not been a good year. My beloved two year old beagle puppy quickly took ill and died of a rare disease, I stumbled, hurting a knee so badly that I would have to have surgery to correct the problem, and most devastatingly, my wife of fifteen years and mother of my two beautiful sons decided she didn't want to be married any longer.

Initially, I had my usual thoughts that I am strong and can get through anything. But as time passed, changes in me started to surface. It started with becoming bitter towards my wife, but quickly led into a distrusting nature of people and a genuine feeling of giving up on the human race. For months I ignored the changes and justified newly developing behaviors on the biblical truths that humans are inherently sinful and then added my own rationalization that therefore they should not be trusted. But as time passed I was becoming not only indifferent to others, but apathetic and even resentful. I began to wallow in self-pity and look sarcastically and distrustingly at others.

In the evenings while at home I would talk and play and enjoy my boys while all the time feeling guilty about the new attitudes developing inside of me. How could I raise two boys to be happy and productive while every day I allowed myself to lose faith in mankind? To me, I was creating a paradoxical existence. How could I tell two boys that I loved them when I didn't love anyone else? I believed I was a tremendous failure to my boys since I was unable to keep my marriage together. I prayed to God and asked him to show me I should keep my faith in mankind, to show me why I should push on to live a good and full life.

I continued on playing the positive role model figure for my children, while bitterness towards everything else and everyone else grew inside me. Many days ended in confusion and turmoil; some with tears and some with anger.

For someone who was successful, proud of his life, wife, and children, it was a very disheartening time. To me, I was a new breed of loser, another divorce statistic whose reason for living a good and full life was now in question for the first time in my life.

One morning I made my usual thirty-minute drive to work, parked the car and began my quarter of a mile walk to the office. I refused to pay for parking, a piece of concrete, at our building, and enjoyed my early morning strolls even though this one would prove a little more challenging. I had numerous items clutched under one arm, to include my attaché, sandwich for lunch, and several books for work. Under the other arm was the crutch I needed for support of my injured knee as I waited my turn for surgery.

As I stepped onto the main street to make my way up to the office a public transportation bus, what we call a Bi-state bus, pulled along side me and the female bus driver pulling the lever to open the accordion doors says to me,

"Where are you going?" Her face was an expression of disbelief that I would try to go anywhere with all those things under one arm and a crutch under the other.

I replied, "I only have a short walk of about one quarter of a mile or so."

"Get in," she replied as if to say you need some help sir. I hesitated.

I told her, "I don't have any change on me, and really, I can make it."

Then, she insisted, "Come on!" She stared incredulously and wasn't going anywhere. I jumped on the bus and she drove me to my destination. Like I said, it wasn't a very long ride. I jumped up on my crutch as she came to a stop and turning looked her straight in the eye.

I calmly said, "That was a real nice thing to do."

She just winked and said, "You have a nice day sir."

I watched the bus drive away and thought to myself that maybe there are a few good people left.

About three days later, with the knee propped up under my desk as I still waited my turn for surgery, and in the midst of some stressful divorce negotiations, the bitterness for my wife was peaking. I was probably at an all time lifetime low. This alone should have shown me how good I'd had it up until then, but my blindness to any thing good was growing stronger.

Unfortunately there was some more bad news. I was in the need of some car repairs, which was just what I needed at this time, additional expenses! Without my wife around, as she has already moved out, I decided to call a new dealer repair shop close to work. I knew they would be expensive but wanted quality work done so I didn't have any problems since I now only had the one car. I called to set up an appointment.

"Hello, this is George," said a solid sounding voice on the other end.

"Yes, I'm calling to see if I can set up an appointment for some car repairs," I replied.

"Sure, what's the problem and when would you like to bring her in," he responded helpfully.

"Anytime after work next week is fine," and I went on to explain what needed to be done.

While anger and distrust of anyone were my normal overriding constant feelings as of late, in a moment of feeling sorry for myself, I went on to say, "Now George, I'm in the midst of a divorce and money is tight so I really need you to take care of me here." I was half joking and half serious and honestly hoped the comment might serve to save me a dollar or two.

He didn't hesitate to respond, "Oh, I'm sorry to hear that and unfortunately, been there, done that!"

"You're divorced?"

"Yes, and with five children involved," he seemed to say with a little sadness in his tone.

I immediately thought to myself, what a loser, as if the number of children you had made you and/or the divorce any worse or better. I really wasn't myself.

But George quickly continued, "So, are you praying for her?"

"Come again," I stuttered.

"Are you praying for her?"

"Her?"

"Your soon to be ex-wife, are you praying for her? You know that if you let that bitterness for her eat away at you, it will kill you?"

Shocked, I said, "I guess you're right."

He continued without any provocation, "When I went through my divorce the bitterness I started building inside of me started destroying me and my relationships with my children. At a low point in my life, a friend of mine told me to pray for my wife. I looked at him like he was nuts. Pray for her! You've got to be kidding. I wished her nothing but the worst! I told him I couldn't pray for her. He told me that the bitterness would kill me and that I had to pray for her. I told him I didn't know if I could do it. He persisted and said even if I didn't feel like it, I must pray for her every day. He said eventually it will come from the heart and a life would be saved; mine!" If it weren't for that advice Steve, and the change in George's tone indicated a real sincerity even discernable even over the phone, "there's no telling where I'd be today." So all I can tell you is to pray for her. There was a momentary silence as if he expected me to say something, but I couldn't. Now, when we going to get that car in here?"

I set up the appointment; hung up the phone and "George the Auto Mechanics" words lingered in my mind the remainder of the day. So, are you praying for her? I guess they lingered mostly because I wasn't.

The following week, after knee surgery and with my now mending knee propped up on a box under my desk, I was on a customer call with a nice lady by the name of Michele. The conversation went on as normal, and I was about to give my usual, "You have a great day" and hang up the phone, when the lady asked a question.

"Before you go I just have to say something that may sound really crazy to you?"

"Well, I've had a pretty crazy year ma'am, go right ahead."

To which she quickly responded, "You sound so much like an ex-boyfriend, its scary," with added emphasis on the scary.

To which I responded, "And was it a good relationship?"

"Oh," she said seemingly a little surprised with my quick response, yes, yes!"

"And your last name would be," I inquired? We both laughed.

"I really sound that much like him," I inquired again?

"Yes, she repeated emphatically, it's really unbelievable."

"And you are married now?"

"Yes," hesitatingly she responded, "I am."

"Well, I hope you married the right boyfriend." We both laughed again. And then, out of nowhere, and I guess once again feeling sorry for myself, I blurted out, "I am in the midst of a divorce. It is pretty emotional and I wouldn't wish this on anyone."

The tone in her voice saddened as she relayed that she was sorry and surprisingly shared, "My husband and I have had some serious talks about divorce and it's scary to think about separating."

I told her, "I'm sorry, I hope it works out." The conversation continued if for nothing else that we immediately felt at ease with each other. I shared that my wife and I were different from the start and while the opposites attract theory may be true, it doesn't last. I shared that we were truly opposites, as I would go run five miles while she watched television. I love to be active while she loved to be inactive. And then, it happened!

My friendly customer reflectively stated, "I appreciate your need to be active, you don't know what I'd give just to have someone to go play tennis with." From that moment on it was like I had been given a friend for life. You see, I was a collegiate scholarship athlete in the game of tennis!

Somewhere in the five-minute span of that conversation, I felt a bond of friendship that for me had never formed so quickly. It was like nothing before I had ever experienced. In the end, I told her to call me if she ever needed someone to talk too. She called the next day, and we talked. I called her several days after that and we talked some more. For the next six months of my life I was given as much inspiration for living as I had ever received from any other person.

It turned out that my new friend had a bigger heart than the state she resided in. Totally through phone conversations, we became good friends. At one of the lowest points in my life I was lifted up by a stranger!

I have heard it said that as we age, we humans create layers, which makes it more difficult for us to reveal our true selves to each other, making it difficult to really care for each other. My friend Michele almost immediately recognized my need for someone to talk to, for someone to care. It was as if she felt the hurt inside of me. More dramatically, she didn't stop and simply recognize, she embraced, she reached out, she gave me hope! I only hope I did the same for her.

To this day, while our lives have taken different courses and we've gone our own ways, I will never forget the many conversations that meant so much to me and never forget her kindness.

These three events that occurred within a two-week period, made me sit back and think.

Out of nowhere, and shortly after some consistent and very sincere praying, three strangers had showed me kindness and even offered guidance needed to get back a good attitude and get a life back on course. I had to question that if God wasn't sending me a message, what other explanation could there be? Still, I remained a doubting Thomas and may have ignored even these clear signs; the "Bus Driver", "George the Auto Mechanic", and "My Friend Michele", if it weren't for what happened next.

I had prayed hard for many months for God to give me a sign that life was worth living that I had not botched it up beyond repair. Better yet, I prayed for a sign that living and giving in this world and to other human beings was really worth it. Even further, as my marriage deteriorated before my eyes, I accepted that I must have let God down in a very big way, and my marriage was my punishment. I had begun to accept a very sad sentiment, namely, that I would never have a wife I truly loved and a relationship anything like it was supposed to be, one where two people truly cared for and about each other. There were nights sleeping next to my now ex-wife in which I truly felt sorry for both of us. I specifically remember one night when I was especially saddened by the unhappiness I had created in my own life. As tears silently rolled down my face I quietly prayed to God. I asked that if I ever were given the chance to have a wife I truly loved all I would ask is that she would take walks with me, so I could hold her hand and we could just talk. I truly just needed someone I could really talk too.

My ex-wife and I did finally divorce after fifteen years of marriage. I felt tremendous guilt, as I know it hurt my two boys that I love with all my heart. They were the ages of thirteen and fourteen at the time, already an emotional period in a young persons life. And now, I was party to inflicting on them more emotional stress caused by my own failure in marriage. I will take any pain I caused them to my grave as one of my biggest failures and I only hope that in some manner it will serve to make them stronger.

About one year after my divorce I had an unexpected and brief conversation with the mother of one of the kids whose son was on the same soccer team as my son. I knew she had recently been through a divorce, and while I really didn't know her very well, I mentioned how I had been through one myself, hoping she would be someone good to talk too. I asked if she didn't mind if I called her just to talk some time. She said I should call her. I did, and one year later we were married.

It's been almost ten years since my divorce and every day with my Kathleen has truly been a blessing. She not only takes walks with me, but she also jogs with me, bikes with me, golf's with me, and even workouts as much as I do. She is pretty, kind, smart, and more than I deserve; she's the finishing touch in the miracle that occurred in my life shortly after I received the signs. I am truly convinced she's one of God's Angels!

When I look back on what happened to me, now almost 10 years ago, I still remember it all as though it happened yesterday; you don't forget miracles easily! At my lowest point, I prayed more than I ever had in my life, for help, for guidance, and mostly for a restoration of my positive attitude and faith in mankind. God sent me three signs and an Angel.

The "Bus Driver" said, "Do little things for people, it makes a difference". "George, the Auto Mechanic" said, "Always pray for your fellow man, we all need each others prayers". "My Friend Michele", said, "Friendship and love are the greatest gifts of all, never give up on these".

And my Kathleen, well she's a gift from God and I'm still trying to figure out why I deserve her. We take walks, hold hands, and talk every day!

What I'm not sure of is whether or not the Angel has been sent to watch over me so I don't fall again, or if this was an Angel here on earth that needed the help of someone who lived through a miracle! It doesn't matter, because I realize now what I should have never doubted. God gives us life to be the best we can be and he created mankind, and I should never question his goals or the goodness of his creations.

THE END!

This book is one of the many products produced by

PROFESSIONAL & PERSONAL LIVING ASSISTANTS, INC.

Professional & Personal Living Assistants, Inc.
is a firm dedicated to assisting individuals in numerous aspects of their lives ranging from job-hunting to professional management efficiency, to personal finances, and more.

Our goal is to assist individuals in being more organized and in control of their lives in order to be happier and more fulfilled!

If you've been happy with our book and are interested in the job hunting services referred to in this book, or any other services,
(our personal budgeting product is very helpful)
then you should visit our website at "PPLAservicesforyou.com".

If you would like to speak with the author,
and/or be interested in any consulting services
please call us at 1-636-477-8801.

978-0-595-41461-1
0-595-41461-3

CPSIA information can be obtained at www.ICGtesting.com
231939LV00002B/23/A